Frank Lloyd

WRIGHT

ROCKPORT

Frank Lloyd

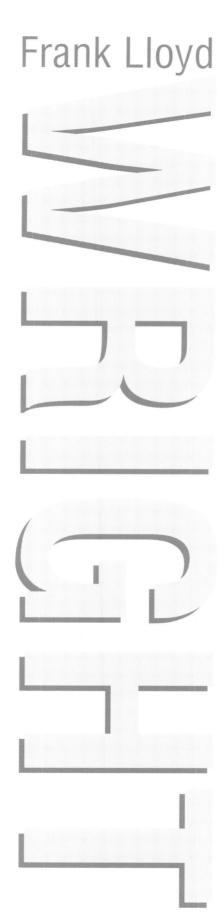

WRIGHT

GLOUCESTER MASSACHUSETTS

ROCKPORT PUBLISHERS

Editor: Sol Kliczkowski

Texts: Aurora Cuito and Sol Kliczkowski

Graphic Design: Emma Termes Parera

Translation: William Bain

Drawings: © 2003 The Frank Lloyd Wright

Foundation, Scottsdale. AZ./VEGAP, Barcelona

Copyright for the international edition:

© H Kliczkowski-Onlybook, S.L.

La Fundición, 15. Polígono Industrial Santa Ana

28529 Rivas-Vaciamadrid. Madrid

Ph.: +34 91 666 50 01

Fax: +34 91 301 26 83

onlybook@onlybook.com

www.onlybook.com

Copyright for the US edition:

© 2003 by Rockport Publishers, Inc.

Published in the United States of America by:

Rockport Publishers, Inc.

33 Commercial Street

Gloucester, Massachusetts 01930-5089

Tel.: (978) 282-9590

Fax: (978) 283-2742

www.rockpub.com

Library of Congress Cataloging-in-Publication Data available

ISBN: 1-59253-009-5

10 9 8 7 6 5 4 3 2 1

Printed in China

Due to the creative and innovative nature of his work, architect Frank Lloyd Wright is considered one of the precursors of contemporary architecture. Wright's prolific oeuvre (more than one thousand buildings) is proof of a diverse inheritance from various avant-garde movements such as Cubism, Expressionism, Arts and Crafts, Art Nouveau, Rationalism, and Minimalism. Wright's work stands out for the way in which it unites new materials and grants functionality to different spaces.

Wright's private life was marked by unfortunate scandals such as the fire that consumed his house, Taliesin East, and caused the death of seven people, among them Mamah Borthwick Cheney, the woman for whom the architect had abandoned his family for a few years earlier. Among the succession of women that accompanied Wright throughout his life there was Miriam Noel, whose mental instability resulted in her incarceration. Despite a turbulent private life, Wright was a tenacious worker, and his career progressed unyieldingly, enriched by experimentation with innovative techniques.

Wright's inclination for architecture began to take shape in early childhood. His primary boyhood pastime was Froebel blocks, invented by the kindergarten pioneer and consisting of a series of spheres, blocks, pyramids, and paper strips. They permitted the young Wright to experiment with multiple combinations, which proved decisive in his spatial and analytical training. A parallel can be drawn from these geometric games and conjugation of elements to the formal character Wright´s design style would later take. Another influence in Wright's development was Unitarianism, a religion that encourages the individual to seek God in the world. This creed, which had an influence on the entire Wright clan, was the nucleus of the architect's personal exploration, a spiritual journey that looked to science and art as the vehicles by which one could come to know God.

Wright's architectural language is noteworthy for the use of geometric elements and horizontal and vertical lines in walls. As a result walls are independent from the interior structure, such as in the Johnson Building (Wisconsin). The resulting breakdown of elements allows the qualities of each element to stand out. Furthermore, the work of the celebrated architect also reflects a Japanese influence.

Within the catalogue of Wright's work there are two kinds of homes, both of his own invention: Prairie houses (1904–1909) and Usonian houses (1939–1940). Wright conceived the first with certain common characacteristics in mind: horizontality; roofs that go beyond the limit established by low walls and longitudinal windows; an elevated groundfloor; an important relation with nature and landscape; and an open layout. Usonian houses, on the other hand, represent a more modern and pragmatic form of expression. Instead of being large spaces to accomodate guests, Usonian homes are smaller and more intimate, designed to meet individual necessity. Wright understood "usonia" as an expression of the ideal life in the United States, and with this notion in mind he conceived the Usonian model. A Usonian home often has *L*-shaped floors. It maintains the open-layout character of the Prairie house while doing away with its more formal aspects. In the Usonian model is also found the utilization of natural materials and ornaments.

The experimentation with different forms inspired Wright to design an integrated furniture ensemble as well as independent pieces, given his belief that "distinct" spaces require "distinct" forms. Color, light, and shadow characterize Wright's buildings. With these resources he was able to create intimate, luminous spaces, in addition to the well-known stained-glass windows that give rise to environments of peculiar character.

There is an ongoing playful dialogue with scale in Wright's work. This is true of the Unity Church and the residences, both of which communicate a dramatic sense of spaciousness, as well as the Morris Store. Spatial conception is one of Wright's main concerns, and different environments are articulated with few separations occurring between them. The ceiling is the element that joins the spaces while always maintaining its own identity, thereby disassociating itself from the whole.

The integration of nature is evident in the use of materials that combine air, water, land, and fire. As can been seen in the Fallingwater House, the Storer House, or the H. C. Price House, the architecture coalesces in the stone, water, and vegetation. In all of these constructions Wright demonstrates complete awareness of spatial determination.

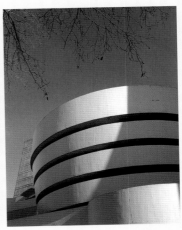

In Gaelic, which was the language of Wright's ancestors, "taliesin" means "bright peak." Wright took this word from Gaelic mythology for the weekend house that he built in 1911. Taliesin would undergo multiple amplifications, renovations, and reconstructions throughout the years, thus becoming the lengthiest project of the architect's life.

The work was born of Wright's need to escape the bustle of Chicago and return to his birthplace. His mother's family, the Wright Jones, had settled in Wisconsin around 1865. Over time the family prospered, accumulating a dozen farms scattered across the region. For one of these plots, Wright designed a bucolic refuge which he later transformed into a residence, studio, and workshop. The structure was enhanced by the restoration of nearby edifices such as a windmill, an old school, and a small restaurant.

Two tragic fires, in 1914 and 1925, respectively, required that Taliesin be almost completely reconstructed. The resulting buildings were christened Taliesin II (1914–1925) and Taliesin III (1925–1959). The one-story structure is strategically placed at the top of a hill from which magnificent views of the landscape can be observed. The materials used were for the most part stone and wood. The exquisite design of all constructive details and meticulous craftmanship resulted in deep formal richness, a great of variety of finishes, and imaginative solutions throughout the work. The above-mentioned preciseness is evident, for example, in the size of the stones (of unequal form and thickness) used in the walls in order to create textured faces. Furthermore, the wood partitions that separate the different rooms consist of strips going in different directions and perforated with small openings that grant the environments a dynamic quality.

As in nearly all of Wright's works, the furniture was designed specifically to satisfy the character and functional necessities of the project.

Location: Spring Green, Wisconsin, US
Date of construction: 1911–1959
Photographer: Scot Zimmerman

8

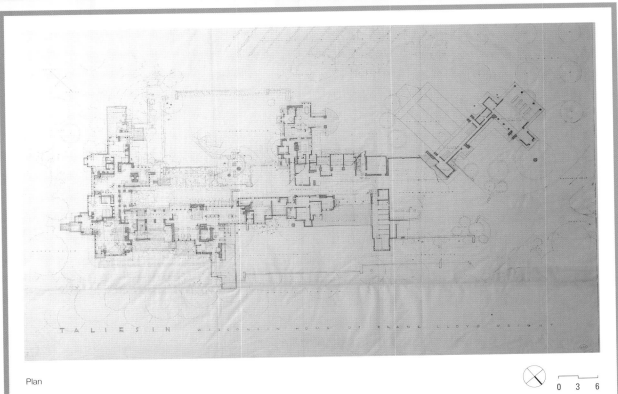

Plan

0 3 6

This project was carried out under the auspices of Aline Barnsdall, heiress to the Barnsdall Oil Company. The goal was to build a complex devoted to the theater. Barnsdall's passion for the theater resulted in the purchase of a vast property in the center of Los Angeles, Olive Hill, at the foot of which a large theater, a cinema, homes for actors and actresses, and several stores and businesses were to be built. At the summit would be Barnsdall's house, Hollyhock. While plans for the theater did not materialize, Barnsdall's house and two others were in fact built.

In 1917, the starting date of construction, Los Angeles was still a desert. It was thus necessary to irrigate and landscape the lot so that it would be more suitable to a tropical setting. Given the intensity of the sun in the region, Wright conceived of a main house with a certain introspective character in place of a residence oriented toward the exterior. To this end, Wright created a tree-covered interior patio to provide the space with shade. He also designed windows of reduced dimension when compared with those of his Prairie homes. Sliding glass doors blur the limits between interiors and exterior.

Wright granted the element of water a prominent role. He created a brook that circulates from a fountain to a large pond on the patio, continuing into the interior of the house in front of the fireplace, and on into a square swimming pool before the living room windows.

In this work, one which Wright himself qualified as a "California romance design," the relationship with nature, harmoniously achieved through large sculpture-like volumes, also appears in the decorative motif of hollyhock—Barnsdall's favorite flower. The flower was used to ornament the windowsills, colonnades, and concrete gardens, as well as the chairbacks that were custom-designed for the house.

While this project proved to be the most difficult of Wright's residential commissions, due as much to the perfectionism of the client as that of the architect himself, he would remember the period with special affection.

Location: Los Angeles, California, US
Date of construction: 1917–1920
Photographer: Scot Zimmerman

Perspective

Over the years the house fell into neglect, as ownership changed on various occasions. Finally, the city of Los Angeles, in collaboration with Wright's son, took responsibility for Hollyhock's restoration.

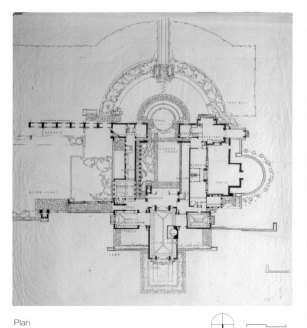

Plan

0   3   6

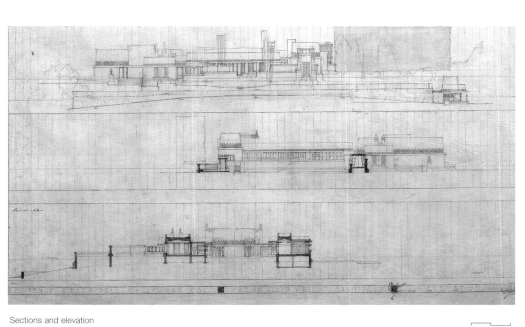

Sections and elevation

0   4   8

This home is one of Frank Lloyd Wright's prefabricated buildings with indigenous granite. In contrast to other designs, here the characteristic and mysterious transition between interior and exterior is not so apparent. The home is situated above street level. Access to the main patio is achieved after ascending two sections of stairs, accompanied by a fountain that terminates in a small swimming pool. On the first facade level, five glass doors alternate with stone-block columns decorated in geometric motifs.

These doors provide direct access to the dining room, which along with the second-floor living room make up the nucleus of the house. The result is a large luminous space in which the walls indicate the geometric configuration of the stone blocks. The home benefits from a north-south orientation. Light enters through windows and glass doors that alleviate the solidity of the stone. The layout of the home gives the spaces considerable mobility and invites fluid circulation between the different levels.

Despite the exterior appearance, the house is arranged in four levels with their own environment and space. The four identical bedrooms are located on the level between the living room and dining room. The dining room and kitchen occupy, along with the wing dedicated to the service rooms and a small room that surrounds the chimney, the first floor. The living room extends across the entire level, with terraces that open to the garden.

With changes in ownership the home underwent varied remodelings. Finally, in 1970, Eric Lloyd Wright, son of the renowned architect, restored the home at the request of the new occupant. Such changes as the installation of electric heat and a new swimming pool were made. Wright's original intention, however, was maintained in the whole, characterized by the balance between the transparency of the glass and the consistency of the stone and the dramatic opening of the home to the exterior.

Location: Hollywood, California, US
Date of construction: 1923
Photographer: Scot Zimmerman

Perspective

The relation with the exterior is present in the rooms. Each has been fitted out with large openings that communicate with terraces and gardens surrounding the home.

The magic of this project resides in the combination of folk and traditional motifs with singular and timeless shapes, which have made it into one of the icons of twentieth century architecture.

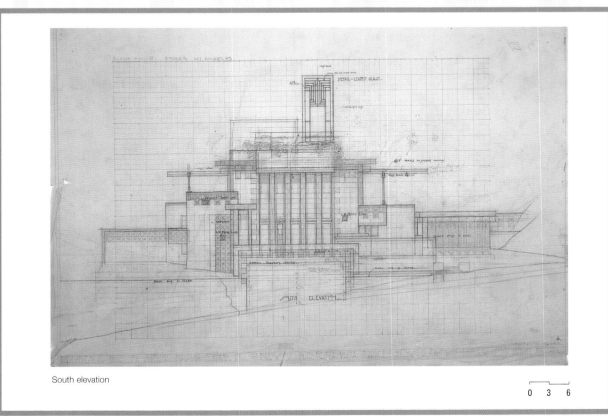

South elevation

0   3   6

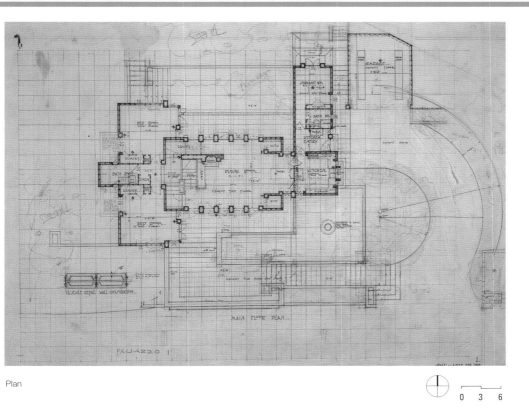

Plan

Of all Wright's constructions, Fallingwater House is the most famous. An elevated building situated on a waterfall, the home sits between the Pennsylvania hills and is adapted perfectly to the form of the rocks.

With this house, Wright sought to join the elements of nature—forest, river, and rock—with the construction materials as much as possible. The goal was to create a building in harmony with the setting and to provide a space for rest and relaxation. The relation with nature is characteristic of Wright's work, yet in this design the architect accentuates the intimacy the occupants share with the vegetation and exterior landscape.

The architect celebrates horizontality by calling attention to the projection of the living room and that of the upper terraces. The main home consists of three stories. The main floor, with two terraces, offers a view in three directions. On the upper floor each of the bedrooms has its own terrace, as do the third-floor study and balcony. A semicircular walk goes from the main house to the guesthouse, situated slightly further up on the hill.

The home is accessed by crossing a small bridge and following a narrow passageway in back of the house. The entrance is small so as to call attention to the ample, luminous living room space to which it gives way. Structure plays a major role here, evidenced by the suspended stairs that lead down to the water level. Dominant architectural moulds are broken to give place to creative freedom at the project's conception.

The vertical elements of the house are of local stone. A certain relief accentuates the sculptural aspect of the whole. The horizontal elements are made of reinforced concrete. The floors and walls are stone-covered, with fine-grained walnut woodwork.

With this project Wright set forth a new design, unlimited by symmetry, walls, geometric schemes, or privileged points of view. Research into structures to maintain the house atop the waterfall advanced at its own pace. The unconventional location of the house has taken its toll in the form of structural problems —in part resolved—which have troubled the home for some years.

Location: Bear Run, Pennsylvania, US
Date of construction: 1935–1939
Photographer: Paul Rocheleau

Thanks to the vast glass surfaces and the use of stone and wood, the interior of the house appears to be an extension of nature in the exterior.

Perspective

In 1936, the year in which Wright designed his first Usonian house (Jacobs Home), Paul and Jean Hanna commissioned the architect to build their new home in northern California. In keeping with the philosophy of low production costs that inspired the creation of Jacobs House, Wright, despite Hanna House's being 3,225 square feet larger than the above mentioned building, was able to limit the budget to the extreme.

With this as well other residential projects undertaken during the period, Wright wanted to resolve what he called the problem of the American house. He wanted to tackle residential projects economically without sacrificing a high standard of comfort. The solution was one-story homes in which skillful use of space, materials and building techniques required neither aesthetic sacrifice nor neglecting the clients' needs. The rooms of the house given the most attention were the living room (spacious and open to the exterior), the kitchen (practical and compact), and a cement flooring to hide the hot water system.

Wright's houses are governed by a modular system. The base of the system is a geometric figure that determines spatial distribution, design of the flooring, the structural system, and which even appears as a decorative element on furniture or lamps.

For Hanna House the hexagon was chosen to emulate honeycombs, objects whose structural flexibility and dynamic form Wright championed. Hexagonal geometric units were applied throughout the home, and the residence came to be known as Honeycomb House. The absence of right angles emphasizes fluidity and movement between the rooms and with the exterior. All of the rooms in the house except for the kitchen open up to landscaped terraces paved with hexagonal tiles.

The Hannas, who had rented the property to the University of Stanford over a long period of time, required adaptability to possible changes in the organization of the rooms. Anticipating the necessities of his clients, Wright designed several vertical wood faces with studs that could easily be withdrawn, thus allowing effortless reconfiguration of the rooms.

Location: Palo Alto, California, US
Date of construction: 1936
Photographer: Scot Zimmerman

The owners altered the arrangement of the house several times, without any sacrifice to the original spirit, before bequeathing the building to Stanford in 1974.

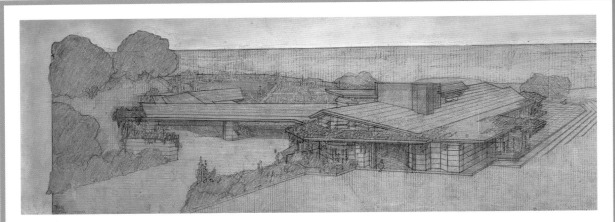

Perspective

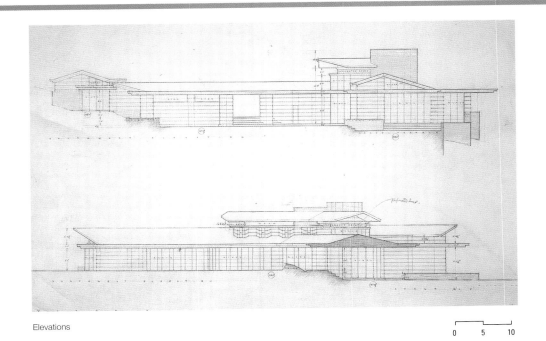

Elevations

0   5   10

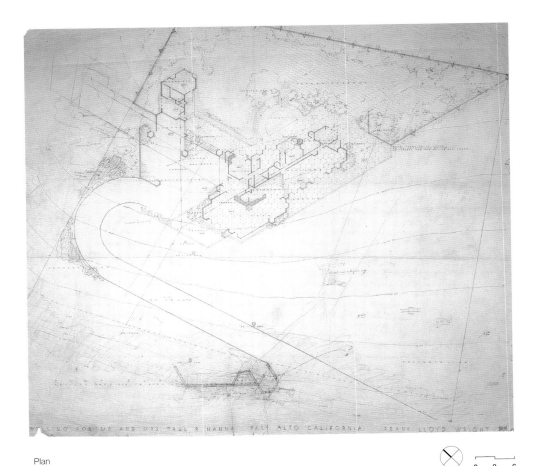

Plan

0   3   6

Following his first trip to Arizona in 1927, Wright reiterated, on several ocassions, his intention to return to the desert region of Sonara as a refuge from the brutal winters of Wisconsin, where he had established a permanent residence. The building is set atop a summit. It served as the home and workplace for the architect, his family, and the apprentices who made up the Taliesin Fellowship, a course for architectural students created by Wright and his third wife Olgivanna, in 1932.

In 1937, Wright decided to buy a lot situated to the northeast of the town of Scottsdale and at the foot of the McDowell mountain range. It was here where Wright and his young disciples designed and built the winter home and studio that would be dubbed Taliesin West. The complex includes residences, drafting rooms, a workshop, a store, and two theaters surrounded by various gardens and terraces.

The project was literally born of the desert. The students collaborated in the collection of local rocks and sand, the primary materials in the construction. The skillful use of indigenous materials results in a perfect integration of the structure with the surrounding landscape. Even the selection of color emphasizes the relation between the building complex and the desert tableland on which the construction is situated.

The complex unfolds along an axis that joins the access area and the leisure zone. A triangular space halfway between these two points contains the workshops, the dining room, and lavatories. All of the rooms open to landscaped terraces with views of the plateau. The homes, almost all of which were designed by the students in an experimental manner, are scattered across the grounds.

The structural system of the complex consists of widestone walls and a roof system in the form of a sequoia-beam framework. White-cloth tensioning remnants between the secondary beams provide the camp-like atmosphere that Wright sought for the complex. Glass panels were installed to reinforce the roofs.

Location: Scottsdale, Arizona, US
Date of construction: 1938–1959
Photographer: Scot Zimmerman

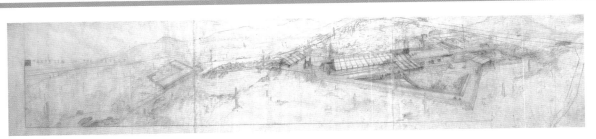

Perspective

Today, Taliesin West, declared a world heritage, is the headquarters of the Frank Lloyd Wright Foundation. The Foundation includes more than seventy architects who work to preserve the architectural legacy of the master.

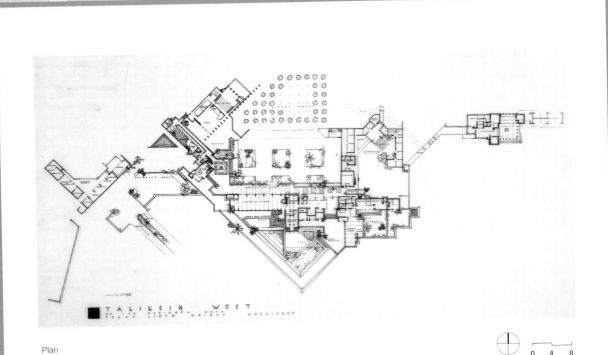

Plan

This construction consists of different buildings arranged asymmetrically but which nonetheless appear in ordered fashion. Here the architect returns to themes of earlier years, revealing a special attraction for sixty and thirty degree angles in order to create geometric forms that assume primacy as much in the structure as in the wall ornamentation.

The access to the Pfeiffer chapel appears in the shadow of a concrete structure that plays with the juxtaposition of forms. In terms of volume, the Pfeiffer chapel consists of a double triangle in the form of a glass-and-concrete diamond. The Roux Library complements the chapel, and its design responds to an imaginary circle of diamonds. Furthermore, the administrative building consists of a double structure united by an intermediary patio. A large grassy zone was designed for the enjoyment and relaxation of the students. The green area also constitutes the unifying point of the complex.

Complications with the plans resulted in postponements in the construction of the university complex during many years. The result was scattered but still harmonious planning. Marked Wrightesque lines are evident throughout the buildings, and the materials used add to the spirit characteristic of the architect. The solidity of the concrete is softened by metal and glass structures and with geometric openings and openwork that permit the passage of light. The drawings and designs on the walls and columns contribute to creating a more volatile image than is customary in solid constructions. The grayish colors are also weakened with the use of red and vivid colors in the garden.

The Florida Southern College complex allowed the architect to demonstrate his creative ability in the form of a distinct Wrightesque urban landscape spread across spacious grounds. The architect knew how to take advantage of this opportunity, and was even able to conceive of an alternative city with an urban design and planning.

Location: Lakeland, Florida, US
Date of construction: 1917–1920
Photographer: Scot Zimmerman

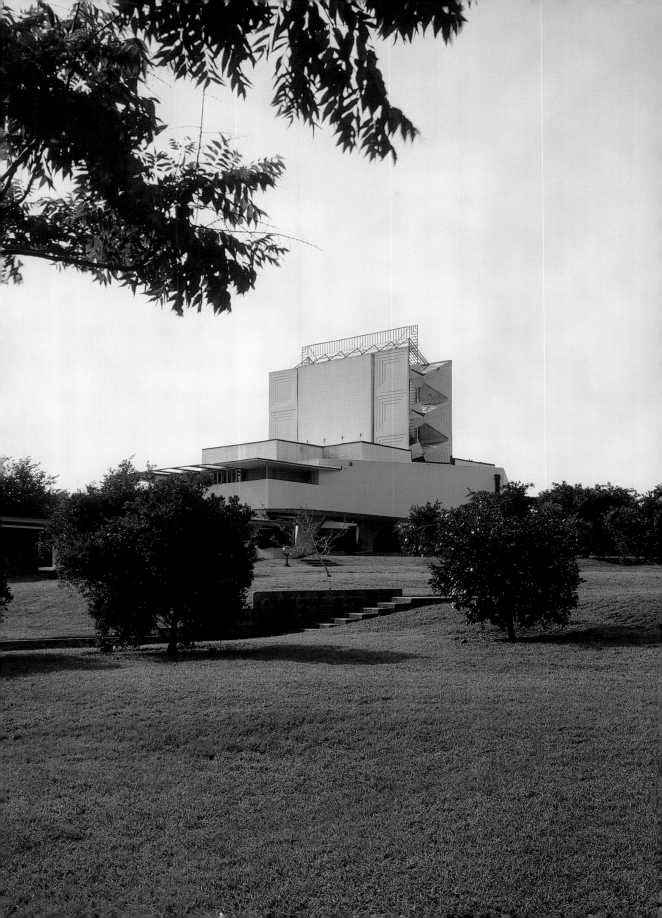

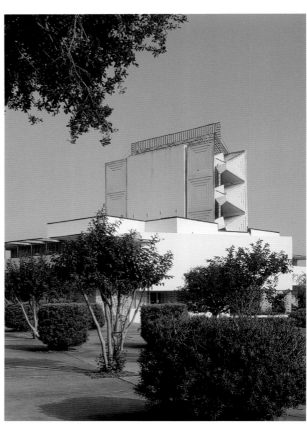

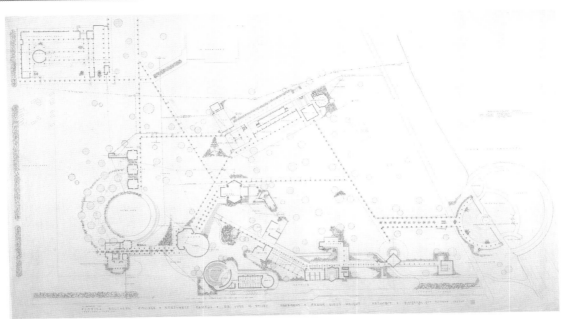

Plan

0   10   20

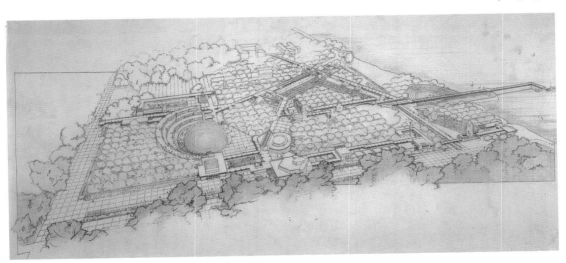

Perspective

The courtyards, the glass windows, the skylights, and the walls with ceramic latticework, create ambiences of diverse lighting and brightness. The sun sneaks in, is filtered, and floods all the nooks and crannies with sunlight.

With this building, Wright proves that a store can grab the attention of clients without the necessity of an elaborate showcase. The project did not require the complete construction of the establishment but rather consisted of remodeling an existing warehouse on a narrow San Francisco street.

The building facade stands out among the neighboring edifices as a result of the horizontal treatment of the bricks. This gave rise to a more striking finish than glass. An asymmetric arch affords a complete view of the interior and welcomes the visitor. The juxtaposition of glass and crystal gives rise to play between notions of solidity and transparency. The visitor is also greeted by a path of lights that run along the wall and beneath the arch, trailing off into the interior.

From the discreet but still monumental facade, access is gained to the large interior space. The interior breaks with the stolid exterior character thanks to a dramatic interplay of forms. A spiral ramp joins the ground floor with the upper level and contributes to opening up the space with a line of movement that follows the formal theme of circles, arches, and curves. This design is heir to the Guggenheim Museum (whose plans date from 1943 but was not built until later), where Wright for the first time utilized the interior ramp as a characteristic element in a building. The ceiling is covered with a framework of plastic concave and convex lamps and the curved walls are decorated with openings and circular ox eyes. A concrete flowerpot continues the convex form of the ceiling and is visible from both levels of the store.

At the request of the client, Wright designed independent furniture, made by Manuel Sandoval, the result of which was to present the items in the gift store in an elegant manner. Round armchairs with cushions and semicircular tables facilitate the selection of items and guarantee the comfort of visitors to the store.

After this project the Morris's commisioned Wright to design three homes that were never built. Today, the store houses an art gallery, allowing the public to appreciate an important legacy of the architect's work.

Location: San Francisco, California, US
Date of construction: 1948–1950
Photographer: Scot Zimmerman

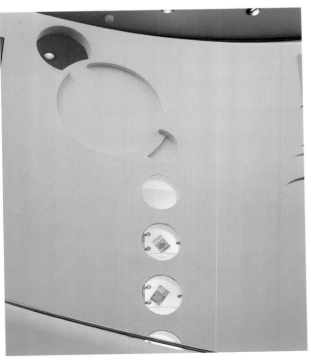

Elevation

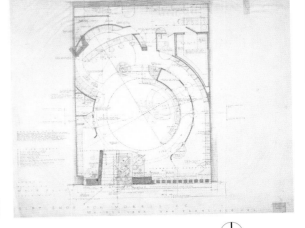

Plan

0 4 8

Great attention to details is manifest all throughout the project, in the choice of materials, the arrangement of the lighting, and in all of the pieces of furniture.

Wright received this commision while he was working on the Price Tower (Bartlesville, 1952) project. It was the result of Harold and Mary Lou Price becoming captivated by the desert region and wanting to build a winter house there to accomodate their five grandchildren. The architect named the building Grandmother House and granted the client special treatment, as Price had already granted Wright the opportunity to build his first skyscraper, the Price Tower.

In this extended narrow construction, Wright demonstrates, once again, that economic materials can give splendid results if employed with mastery. To this end a concrete block becomes a sculptural element that grants the walls personality, while metal is used to complement the block. Wright employed concrete columns that do not reach the roof and are supported by a series of hollow narrow pillars, forming a rectilinear structure that goes over the walls to the house. The pillars are equipped with lighting, thus emphasizing this floating effect.

The covered patio was designed with the children and enjoyment of the exterior space in mind. It was equipped with a fountain and a fireplace for more warmth. The entire house was designed with the children in mind. To this end the western side of the home, the direction toward which the house inclines, was fitted out with a swimming pool surrounded by a landscaped zone. Later, when the children had grown up, all the play zones and rooms were adapted in conformity with the necessities of the house.

Access to the home is granted via a long staggered corridor and coincides with a central patio. Bedrooms on one side and a living-dining room on the other entail the interior distribution. Another wing contains the service rooms and garage. Simple lines inscribing the design of the house are apparent in the combination of walls and concrete columns, in the metal pillars, and in the horizontality of the etched copper-sheet roof. All of the details evidence the architect's originality. While in this period the work of artisans proved to be economically impractical, Wright was nonetheless able to make his own creative language stand out through the intelligent union of architectural elements.

Location: Scottsdale, Arizona, US
Date of construction: 1955
Photographer: Scot Zimmerman

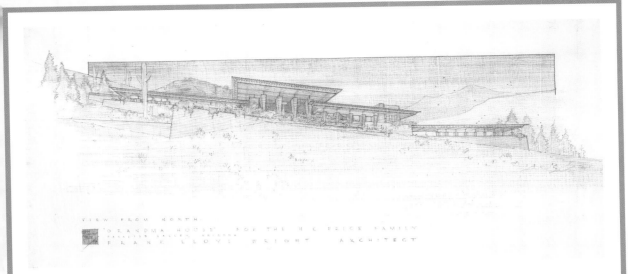

Perspective

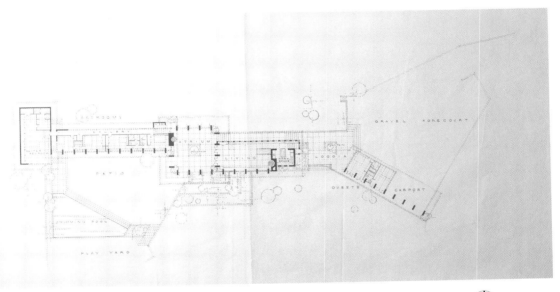

Plan

The lineal arrangement of the rooms
affords each of them a privileged view
of the landscape of terraces, balconies,
courtyards, and their own porches.

With this work Wright culiminated his career, moving closer to a city which traditionally views the innovative tendencies of western-based movements such as the Chicago school with a certain reticence.

The project was very polemical in that it constituted, to a certain degree, a musuem with a continous trajectory, in opposition to the box-room design characteristic of traditional museums. Controversy also surrounded the relation the building would have to the city. Wright proposed a spiral, open to the urban space and presenting the structural interior with clarity. In place of conventional leveling the interior would consist of a ramp.

Wright′s idea was that the visitor to the museum would ascend by elevator to the upper level and gradually descend via the ramp around an open patio. In this way the visitor could go up or down by elevator from all levels and arrive at the end of the exhibition on the ground floor, close to the exit. Guggenheim liked the idea and supported it energetically, until his death in 1949. Notwithstanding, commencement of work was postponed due to changes in site conditions and museum plans, as well as rising material costs. At the time of the architect's death, the museum was practically completed. Only some final details were left unfinished.

The controversy unleashed by the musuem also penetrated artistic circles. Some artists argued that the inclining walls and the ramp were not conducive to the proper exposition of paintings. In response, Wright argued that by slightly inclining the walls, the paintings actually benefitted from the resulting improvement in perspective and lighting. This powerful work of architecture stands out for the majesty of forms that contain a diverse range of artistic works, thus establishing a symbolically intriguing dialogue between container and content.

When asked what was his most important building, Wright answered "The next one." From this we perhaps may deduce that the Guggenheim Museum, which was his last, was, at least for the architect, his principal achievement.

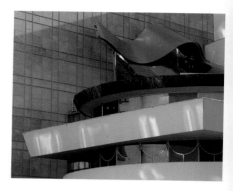

Location: New York City, New York, US
Date of construction: 1955–1959
Photographer: Pep Escoda

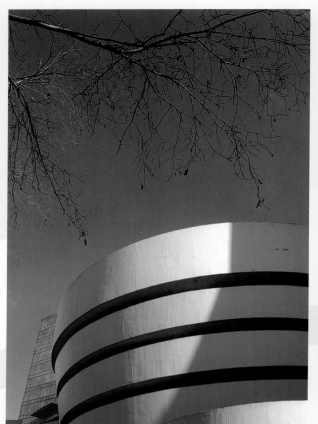

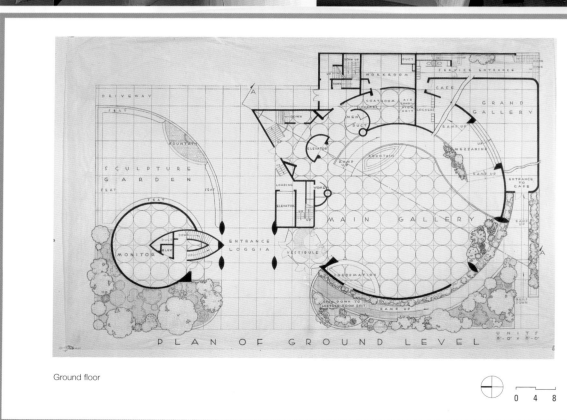

Ground floor

PLAN OF GROUND LEVEL

UNITS
8'-0" X 8'-0"

0 4 8

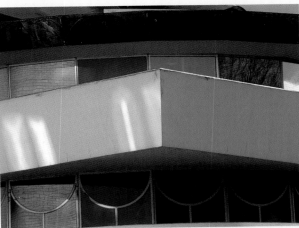

Perspective

Interior perspective

Wright was already advanced in years when he took on his first and only governmental commission, a new civic center in San Rafael, to the north of San Francisco. The site was a vast park with a lake and small hills on which the architect set the building, adapting the construction to the configuration of the landscape and imperfections in the terrain.

However, Wright did not allow himself to be limited by setting. As is apparent in the two wings of the building flanked by a pair of hills, Wright incorporated nature into the design. One of these wings contains the administrative department while the other the courthouse. From both, views of the interior garden and lake can be observed.

In contrast with other official buildings, the Marin County Civic Center maintains a human scale, making constant reference to the landcape and surrounding nature. This quality is also characteristic of the interior. Between the two main buildings runs a landscaped walk illuminated by glass ceilings.

The whole stands out for its exuberant and playful aspect, qualities which are not usually associated with this type of construction. Wright joins circles, spheres, or semicircles in structural and decoratiove combinations, in this way highlighting the configuration of the curved forms that identify the construction. The decoration becomes, as Wright himself stated, an integral part of the building. From the exterior of the building this gives rise to a highly energetic visual rhythm, with changes in the proportion of arches and openings from level to level. A central patio functions as a communcating axis for all the levels and the nucleus around which the succession of various offices extends. The walls and partitions were granted mobility so that they could be adpated to the spatial necessity of each department.

The materials utilized, such as the concrete structure and steel, harmonize with the setting as much by virtue of their color as by their placement.

Location: San Rafael, California, US
Date of construction: 1917–1920
Photographer: Scot Zimmerman

Before his death, Wright completed the drawings and plans for the civic center, and Aaron Green, who was involved in the project as associate architect from the outset, Wesley Peters, and Taliesin Associated Architects completed the main building in stages.

The remaining structures were either left unbuilt or constructed along lines that did not follow the original model.

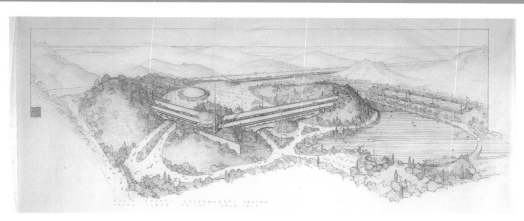

Perspective

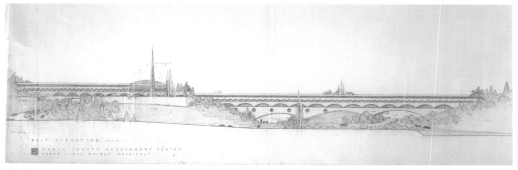

Elevation

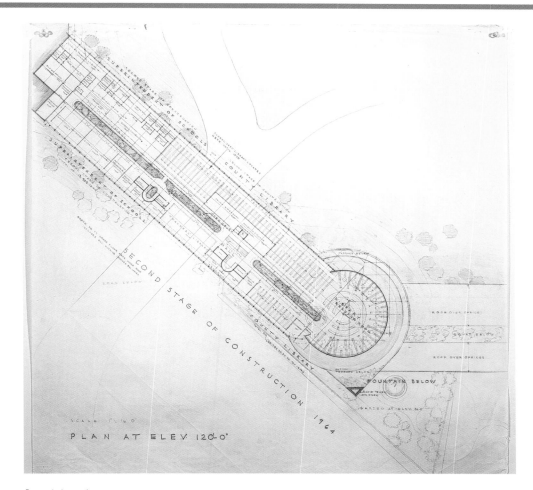

Second phase plan

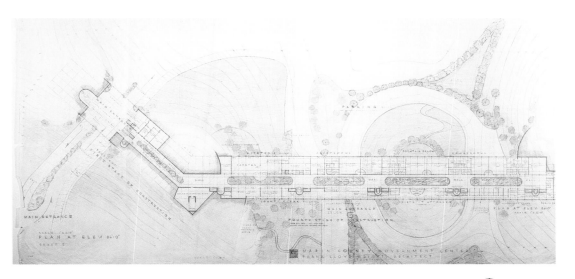

First phase plan

0   5   10

Ablin Residence

The front door to the Ablin home consists of a profiled framework of black-painted steel and several reddish panels. This contrasts the intense verdure of the surrounding vegetation and alludes to the geometry and constructive sensibility that dominate the design as a whole. Beside a wrought-iron gate, and in homage to Wright's work, there was placed a steel sculpture created by one of the architect's admirers. This skillful juxtaposition reveals the artistic tastes of George and Millie Ablin, who commisioned Wright for the project with the conviction that he would know how to join their aesthetic sensibility with the practical and functional necessities of a home.

Having already built two houses in the area, the Fawcett House and the Walton House, Wright was familiar with the terrain and climate of the zone. As such he made use of certain techniques that previously had served him well. Examples are the large inclining roofs to shield the home and the strategic placement of terraces and exterior passages.

Materials and finishing were selected in conformity with the setting. From the reddish color of the concrete on the terraces to the pink hue of the prefabricated blocks for the walls, the materials change tones according to the inicidence of light.

The distribution of the house follows the theoretical precepts and practices that Wright abided by in all of his domestic works, only more evolved in later projects such as this one. The heart of the home is raised on concrete blocks and contains the living room, kitchen, and dining room. The bedrooms form a separate constructive body; in between, multiple patios and terraces permit direct access to the exterior from nearly all the rooms of the house.

The furniture was also designed by Wright, and has barely been altered over the years. The chairs, table, upholstered armchairs, and shelves make up a harmonious ensemble beyond the confines of time and styles. In addition, the die cut of the panels is transparent when light is required and opaque when needed only for decorative purposes, providing a warm personalized air to the rooms in the daytime.

Location: Bakersfield, California, US
Date of construction: 1958
Photographer: Scot Zimmerman

Perspective

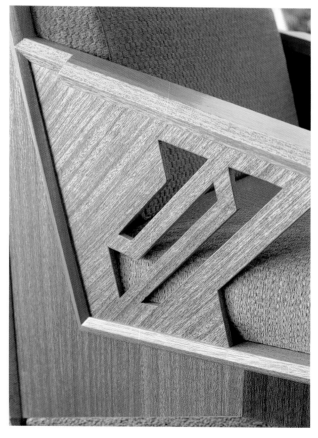

Despite the fact that the project dates from the 1950s, the design seems thoroughly contemporary and has gone beyond the comings-and-goings of fashions and artistic trends. Even the furniture has borne well the passing of time and has inspired numerous present-day artists.

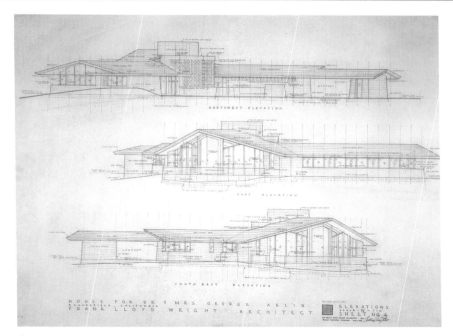

Elevations

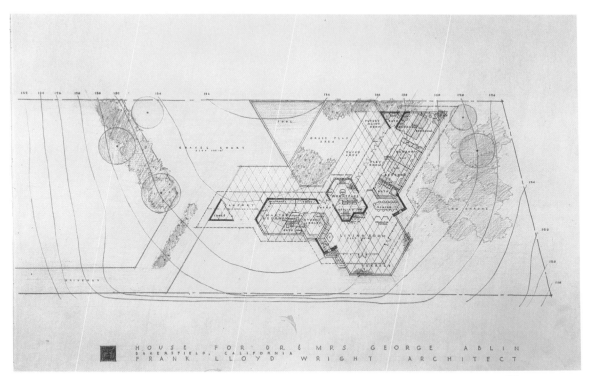

Ground floor

0 5 10

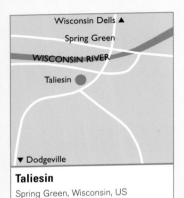

Taliesin

Spring Green, Wisconsin, US

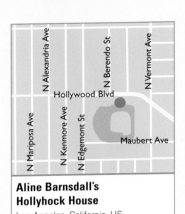

Aline Barnsdall's Hollyhock House

Los Angeles, California, US

Storer Residence

Hollywood, California, US

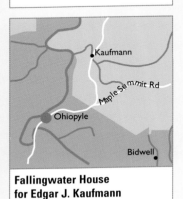

Fallingwater House for Edgar J. Kaufmann

Bear Run, Pennsylvania, US

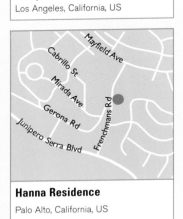

Hanna Residence

Palo Alto, California, US

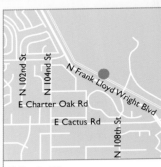

Taliesin West

Scottsdale, Arizona, US

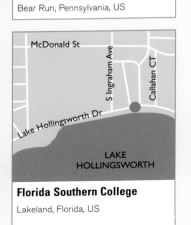

Florida Southern College

Lakeland, Florida, US

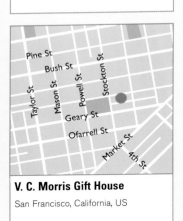

V. C. Morris Gift House

San Francisco, California, US

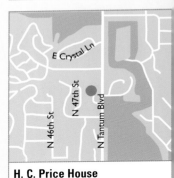

H. C. Price House

Scottsdale, Arizona, US

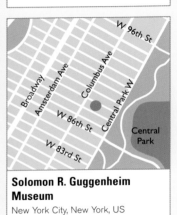

Solomon R. Guggenheim Museum

New York City, New York, US

Marin County Civic Center

San Rafael, California, US

Ablin Residence

Bakersfield, California, US

Chronology of Works

1869	Born in Richland Center, Wisconsin, US
1885	Begins work as a designer in the studio of Allen D. Conover
1887-1893	Works for various studios, among them Adler and Sullivan, until starting his own
1888	House of the architect, Oak Park, Illinois, US
1893	House and painting studio for William H. Winslow, River Forest, Illinois, US
1902	House for W. W. Willits, Highland Park, Illinois, US
	House for Susan Lawrence Dana and Lawrence Memorial Library, Springfield, Illinois, US
	House for Arthur Heurtley, Oak Park, Illinois, US
1904	Headquarters of Larkin Company Administration, Buffalo, New York, US. (No longer standing)
1905	First trip to Japan
1905	Unity Church, Oak Park, Illinois, US
1908	House for Frederick G. Robie, Chicago, Illinois, US
	House for E. E. Boynton, Rochester, New York, US
	House for Meyer May, Grand Rapids, Michigan, US
1911	Taliesin, house-studio of the architect, Spring Green, Wisconsin, US. (Destroyed in 1914)
1915	Imperial Hotel, Tokyo, Japan. (Destroyed in 1968)
1916	House for G. C. Bogk, Milwaukee, Wisconsin, US
1917	Hollyhock House for Aline Barnsdall, Olive Hill, Los Angeles, California, US
1923	Storer House, Hollywood, California, US
1937	Fallingwater House for Edgar J. Kaufmann, Bear Run, Pennsylvania, US
	S. C. Johnson and Son Administration Buildings, Racine, Wisconsin, US
	House for Paul R. and Jean Hanna, Palo Alto, California, US
1938	House for H. Jacobs, Madison, Wisconsin, US
	House for Herbert F. Johnson (Wingspread), Wind Point, Wisconsin, US
1939	Taliesin West, with theater, music pavilion, and Sun Cottage, Paradise Valley, Arizona, US
	Florida Southern College for Dr. Ludd Spivey, Lakeland, Florida, US
1940	Two cottages and house for C. Leigh Stevens, Yemassee, South Carolina, US
1944	Tower for Johnson Wax Company laboratories, Racine, Wisconsin, US
	Design for house for Arnold Friedman (The Fir Trees), Pecos, New Mexico, US
1946	Design for house for V. C. Morris, San Francisco, California, US
1948	House for H. T. Mossberg, South Bend, Indiana, US
	Morris Gift House, San Francisco, California, US
1949	House for Kenneth Laurent, enlarged in 1956, Rockford, Illinois, US
1950	House and guest house for David Wright, Phoenix, Arizona, US
	House for Wiliam Palmer, Ann Arbor, Michigan, US
1954	House for G.B. Tonkens, Amberley Village, Ohio, US
1955	House for H. C. Sr., Paradise Valley, Arizona, US
	Solomon R. Guggenheim Museum, New York City, US
1956	Price Bartlesville Tower, Oklahoma, US
1957	Public administration building and courthouse for the Marin County Civic Center, San Raphael, California, US
1958	House for Don M. Stromquist, Bountiful, Utah, US
	House for George Ablin, Bakersfield, California, US
1959	Synagogue Beth Sholom, Elkins Park, Pennsylvania, US
	Dies 9 April in Phoenix, buried in Taliesin, Spring Green, Wisconsin, US